African AMERICANS

SPIRIT
of America®

African AMERICANS

By Michael Burgan

Content Adviser: Royce Kinniebrew, Museum Teacher,
Charles H. Wright Museum of African American History

The Child's World®
Chanhassen, Minnesota

7

African AMERICANS

Published in the United States of America by The Child's World®
PO Box 326 • Chanhassen, MN 55317-0326 • 800-599-READ • www.childsworld.com

Acknowledgments
The Child's World®: Mary Berendes, Publishing Director

For Editorial Directions, Inc.: E. Russell Primm, Editorial Director; Sarah E. De Capua and Pam Rosenberg, Line Editors; Elizabeth K. Martin, Assistant Editor; Olivia Nellums, Editorial Assistant; Susan Hindman, Copy Editor; Joanne Mattern, Proofreader; Matthew Messbarger, Ann Grau Duvall, and Deborah Grahame, Fact Checkers; Tim Griffin/IndexServ, Indexer; Cian Loughlin O'Day, Photo Researcher; Linda S. Koutris, Photo Selector

Photos
Cover/frontispiece: University of Virginia, Jackson Davis Collection

Cover photographs ©: Corbis

Interior photographs ©: Bettmann/Corbis: 6, 14, 16, 21, 22, 24, 26; Corbis: 7, 9 (Christie's Images), 15, 19, 27 (Reuters NewMedia, Inc.), 28 (AFP); Getty Images/Hulton Archive: 8, 11, 17, 20; Schomburg Center from Research in Black Culture, New York Public Library: 10, 13.

Registration
The Child's World®, Spirit of America®, and their associated logos are the sole property and registered trademarks of The Child's World®.

Library of Congress Cataloging-in-Publication Data
Burgan, Michael.
  African Americans / by Michael Burgan.
    p. cm. — (Our cultural heritage)
  "Spirit of America."
Includes bibliographical references (p.) and index.
  ISBN 1-59296-012-X (alk. paper)
  1. African Americans—Juvenile literature. I. Title. II. Series.
  E185.B95 2003
  973'.0496073—dc21
                            2003004284

14   19   27

Contents

Chapter ONE	*Few by Choice*	6
Chapter TWO	*Slave Life*	10
Chapter THREE	*Struggles of a Free People*	16
Chapter FOUR	*Contributions in Many Fields*	22
	Time Line	29
	Glossary Terms	30
	For Further Information	31
	Index	32

Few by Choice

OVER HUNDREDS OF YEARS, MILLIONS OF Africans have settled in the United States. They created a unique African-American culture. This culture has blended the beliefs and habits from their homeland with the culture of white Europeans who had come to America. Over the years, African-American culture has also shaped how whites lived.

Some of the first African immigrants to America came freely. When the Spanish began building the town of St. Augustine in Florida, in the mid-1560s, the skilled African craftsmen who helped were free. Other immigrants were

St. Augustine, Florida, a city built by the Spanish with the help of free African craftspeople

indentured servants.
Most Africans, however,
arrived in America as
slaves, having been
captured and forced to
work for others against
their will.

The Civil War and
changes to the Consti-
tution ended slavery in
the United States.
However, African-
Americans continued to
face legal and personal
discrimination. Today,
prejudice still exists,
forcing many African-Americans to fight
inequality. Many black Americans, however,
have achieved great success in politics, medicine,
business, sports, and the arts. They have won
legal rights and opportunities that did not exist
even 50 years ago.

In the 1500s, the Spanish and Portuguese
began bringing African slaves to their colonies in
North and South America. The slaves belonged
to many different **ethnic groups** and spoke a

*To protest discrimination,
African-Americans and other
concerned Americans orga-
nized marches in the 1950s
and 1960s.*

7

Many of the first slaves who came to what is now the United States worked on tobacco plantations.

variety of languages. Later, other Europeans, such as the British and Dutch, took part in the slave trade with African nations.

In what is now the United States, many of the first slaves worked in the South, raising tobacco. Later, Southern slaves also raised rice and cotton. In 1619, a Dutch trader sold Africans to the English colonists of Jamestown, Virginia. Over time, all 13 British colonies had slaves. Through the 1700s and 1800s, the lives of slaves—and free blacks, as well—varied greatly, depending on where they lived. Whether slave or free, however, African-Americans were denied the rights that European Americans enjoyed.

WHEN THE SLAVE trade with Europeans began, two powerful African empires were Songhai and Benin. Songhai, centered in what is now Mali, was known for its fine schools and its gold. Benin, to the south of Songhai, produced cloth that was popular in Europe. This empire was also a major source of pepper. Throughout the empires of West and North Africa, slavery was common—as it had been in many parts of the world for thousands of years. Rather than killing defeated enemies, armies often took soldiers and civilians as slaves. Countries sometimes traded their slaves for goods they could not produce on their own.

9

Chapter Two

Slave Life

Enslaved Africans were considered property and sold at auction.

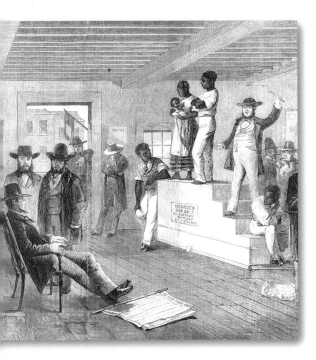

THROUGH THE 1700S SLAVERY GREW RAPIDLY, especially in the South. Farmers did not have enough workers to raise tobacco and other crops sold overseas. Slaves provided this labor. They also held a variety of other jobs throughout the colonies. Some slaves lived in cities, working as servants for whites. Others provided unskilled labor, such as loading and unloading ships. A smaller number of slaves had skilled jobs, such as those of carpentry and shipbuilding.

Although most whites considered African-Americans **inferior,** they accepted some parts of African culture. Africans introduced European Americans to the banjo.

They also taught whites how to prevent smallpox through **inoculation.** The African influence was particularly strong in the South. African slaves brought black-eyed peas to North America, and their cooking styles appeared in many Southern kitchens. The name of a popular Southern dish, gumbo, comes from an African word.

Even as slaves, Africans tried to keep as many of their traditions as possible. This painting shows a group of enslaved Africans celebrating a wedding.

Religion played a large modern role in Africans' lives. African-American slaves tried to preserve the beliefs and **rituals** of their native religions. Some Africans had been Muslims in their homelands. Others followed religions that honored dead relatives and spirits living in nature. During the 1700s, some whites began teaching Christian beliefs to slaves. Many African-Americans then combined a belief in Jesus Christ with some of the rituals of their native faiths. The role of music, clapping, and shouting in many black churches has roots in African religions.

By the time the American Revolution (1775–1783) began, the slave population had reached about 500,000. The war for independence from Great Britain affected the lives of many slaves. A few white Americans believed it was wrong to talk about their own freedom while keeping African-Americans in bondage. Others said slavery went against Christian teachings and called for its **abolition.** The war also gave some slaves a chance to earn their freedom. Both the British and the Americans freed slaves who fought for their side during the war.

After the war, however, U.S. leaders did not address the issue of ending slavery. The Southern states believed they could not survive without slaves. In 1790, the country had almost 700,000 slaves. Around that time, most Northern states began to gradually outlaw slavery.

In the South, though, slavery became even more important. The main reason for this was the invention of the cotton gin in 1793. This device made it easy to remove seeds from cotton. During the 1800s, Southern farmers began planting huge amounts of cotton for the first time. The **plantation** owners relied on slaves to do the hard job of raising and picking the cotton. Without the slaves, these huge crops could not be managed. "King Cotton" became the most important crop in the South, and political leaders fought any efforts to limit slavery.

Meanwhile, in the North, abolitionists began calling for an end to slavery. They demanded that slavery at least be outlawed in new states joining the Union. The abolitionist movement included some free African-Americans, such as Frederick Douglass. He was a former slave who published a newspaper and spoke out against slavery.

The fight to limit or end slavery angered many Southerners who insisted they had a right to own slaves. As politicians debated the issue, many African-Americans acted on their own. They fled their masters and headed to Northern states or into Canada. Some slaves fled to the West or into Florida.

African-Americans paying their respects to Frederick Douglass after his appointment as U.S. marshal for the District of Columbia

13

Some Northern whites and former slaves, such as Harriet Tubman, helped the African-Americans gain their freedom. The people who helped the escaping slaves formed the Underground Railroad. To end this system for aiding slaves, Southern lawmakers pushed for a new law. The Fugitive Slave Act of 1850 forced the quick return of any escaped slaves who were caught in the North.

Slave owners received another boost in 1857, with the *Dred Scott* case. Scott, a slave, had tried to win his freedom through the legal system. In the end, the U.S. Supreme Court ruled that no African-American, slave or free, could be a U.S. citizen, though they could be citizens of an individual state. The Court also ruled that slaves were property and that the government could not ban slavery in U.S. territories. The decision angered abolitionists. Many Americans feared that the North and South were heading toward war.

Harriet Tubman (left) with some of the African-Americans she helped to escape from.

FROM THE EARLIEST DAYS OF THE COLONIAL PERIOD THROUGH THE CIVIL WAR, there were free African-Americans. Some had been indentured servants who completed their service. Some slaves won their freedom by escaping. Other slaves were released by their masters.

Free African-Americans lived in both the North and the South. Although better off than slaves, free blacks still faced laws that limited their freedoms and kept them poor. These laws grew tougher during the 1800s. In the South, blacks could be sold into slavery if they owed money and could not pay. Across the country, free African-Americans could not run for political office, vote, or own guns. Despite the prejudice they faced, some blacks did well. Frances Ellen Watkins Harper (right) was a successful writer and poet. Other free blacks owned farms and businesses. They started their own churches and social organizations. Some free African-Americans even owned slaves and indentured servants.

Chapter THREE

Struggles of a Free People

Abraham Lincoln taking the presidential oath of office at his first inauguration

IN THE 1860 PRESIDENTIAL ELECTION, SLAVERY was the major issue. Abraham Lincoln wanted to stop the spread of slavery in new states. With Lincoln's election, however, most Southerners feared that slavery would be completely wiped out. Eleven Southern states broke away from the United States and created the Confederate States of America. Lincoln would not accept this bold move to break apart the Union. In April 1861, the Civil War began.

For African-Americans, the war was a chance to destroy slavery forever. Many eagerly rushed to join the Northern army. At first, the government was not ready to accept them,

Many African-Americans fought proudly for the Union during the Civil War.

but by the end of the war, nearly 200,000 blacks fought for the Union. Slaves also helped the war effort in the South, transporting supplies and performing other war-related duties. Some slaves, however, took advantage of the war to escape to freedom.

In 1863, President Lincoln signed the Emancipation Proclamation. In this document, he emancipated, or freed, slaves held in Confederate states. In the North, free African-Americans celebrated wildly. For Southern slaves, however, the proclamation meant little. Their freedom would come only when the North won the war. The war continued for two more years after Lincoln's proclamation. The South finally admitted defeat on April 9, 1865. The Northern victory meant that 4 million African-Americans were free for the first time in their lives. Slavery was officially outlawed when the Thirteenth Amendment to the U.S. Constitution was ratified in December 1865.

With the war over, the U.S. government faced two difficult jobs—rebuilding the South and helping blacks adjust to their new freedom. The Fourteenth Amendment made it clear that

Interesting Fact

▶ Sojourner Truth was born into slavery. But after gaining her freedom, she became a traveling preacher. She spoke out about the unfair treatment of both blacks and women. After the Civil War, she worked to help freed slaves.

African-Americans were citizens of the United States. It prevented state governments from denying citizens, especially African-Americans, their **civil rights.**

The years from 1865 to 1877 are known as the Reconstruction Era. During Reconstruction, African-Americans played an active role in U.S. politics for the first time. The first black member of Congress was elected in 1868. Free blacks and former slaves served in Washington, D.C., and in Southern state governments. African-Americans also set up their own colleges, such as Howard University in Washington, D.C., and Hampton Institute in Virginia.

Eventually, however, whites regained control of politics in the South. Despite the Fourteenth Amendment, they made it almost impossible for African-Americans to vote. Southern lawmakers also **segregated** blacks and whites in public. The segregation laws were called "Jim Crow" laws. Jim Crow was a white actor in a popular stage show. He put on black makeup and made fun of African-Americans. In 1896, the U.S. Supreme Court ruled that Jim Crow laws were legal. In the South, then, black children could not attend the same schools as whites. African-Americans could not ride on trains with whites, use the same hospitals as whites, or stay in the same hotels.

During World War I (1914–1918), many African-Americans began leaving the farms of the South. They headed north to large cities, where they could get better jobs. The period from World War I to the end of World War II (1939–1945) is known as the Great Migration. The wars created a demand for many goods, and factories needed more workers. African-Americans, however, sometimes had problems in their new homes. They faced prejudice. In several cities, whites attacked and killed some blacks. These riots, however, were not common.

Starting in the early 1900s, more African-Americans were demanding their civil rights. In 1909, a group of blacks and whites founded the National Association for the Advancement of Colored People (NAACP). One of its leaders was W. E. B. DuBois, a great thinker and writer. The struggle to end segregation and win equality was called the civil rights movement. This movement became more

Two African-American women working in a factory during World War II. Many black Americans moved to large cities to find better jobs during the early 1900s.

19

Interesting Fact

▶ Beginning in 1963, artist and author Faith Ringgold created a series of paintings called American People. These pieces of art looked at the civil rights movement from a female point of view.

The NAACP was founded in 1909. Its members worked hard to help end segregation, and they continue to fight for equal rights for all citizens of the United States.

powerful after World War II. Joined by some whites, blacks began marching in southern cities to protest segregation. They also used the court system to challenge laws that were unfair.

A major victory came in 1954. The Supreme Court ruled that segregation was illegal. Southern states were slowly forced to **integrate** schools and public buildings. Other great achievements came during the 1960s. Congress passed civil rights laws that guaranteed everyone's right to vote. The laws also gave African-Americans and other **minorities** equal rights in schools and in the workplace.

Each new civil rights law gave African-Americans more equality. Blacks won important positions in government, business, and education. Yet many still faced discrimination and prejudice. By the beginning of the 21st century, African-Americans were twice as likely as whites to live in poverty. The struggle for true equality in all parts of life continues today.

IN 1955, A BLACK WOMAN NAMED Rosa Parks sat down on a Montgomery, Alabama, bus. When a white man needed a seat, Parks refused to move for him, as blacks were expected to do. That one small action is sometimes called the start of the modern civil rights movement. Parks was arrested for not giving up her seat, and blacks in Montgomery began a **boycott** against the bus system. One of the leaders of the boycott (left) was the Reverend Martin Luther King Jr. He soon became the best-known leader of the fight for civil rights.

King and his followers used nonviolent marches to promote civil rights. Sometimes, however, the marches turned violent. In 1963, Birmingham, Alabama, police attacked protesters with dogs, clubs, and blasts of water from fire hoses. A few months later, King gave a famous speech in Washington, D.C. Addressing about 200,000 people, King said he dreamed of a day when all Americans would be treated equally.

King was killed in 1968, but other civil rights leaders carried on his work. One of them, Jesse Jackson, twice ran for president. The civil rights movement also spread beyond African-Americans. Other minorities, such as Hispanics and Native Americans, began demanding equal rights. Today, the United States honors King with a national holiday in January. Many Americans remember his brave work and seek new ways to reach his goal of equality for all.

Contributions in Many Fields

Charlie Parker was a famous jazz saxophonist, composer, and bandleader.

AFRICAN-AMERICANS IN THE UNITED STATES HAVE shown an ability to overcome the hardships their ancestors endured. For more than 400 years, blacks have shaped American culture in positive ways.

Music was a key part of African daily life, and it remains an important part of black culture. Yet African-American musical forms go far beyond the black community. Many of the world's most popular musical styles were created by African-Americans. The songs that slaves sang in the fields led to the development of gospel music. These early songs also led to a style called the blues, which later helped shape rock and roll. Early blues greats included Bessie Smith and Robert

Johnson. In rock, Chuck Berry was one of the biggest influences on white musicians.

Another musical style based in the blues is jazz. The masters of jazz include trumpeters Louis Armstrong and Miles Davis, sax players Charlie Parker and John Coltrane, and composer Duke Ellington. Present-day black jazz stars include trumpeter Wynton Marsalis and saxophonist Joshua Redman.

Today, some of the most popular music around the world is rap and hip-hop. The rhymes of rap and pulsing beats of hip-hop came out of black neighborhoods. As hip-hop has developed, it has combined features from other African-American musical styles. Some of the best black rappers have included Tupac Shakur and Jay-Z.

African-Americans have also excelled in other areas of entertainment. At one time, they were not allowed on stages with whites. Whites played black characters by putting on black makeup. During the 1930s and 1940s, producers made films with African-American actors just for black audiences. Few black actors appeared in major films. However, a number of talented black actors finally had a chance to perform on stage and screen. Film actors include James Earl Jones, Denzel Washington, Halle Berry, and Samuel L. Jackson. In television, comedian Bill Cosby starred in one of the most popular shows of all time. On Broadway, stars such as Ossie Davis, Ben Vereen, and Brian Stokes Mitchell have entertained millions over the years.

In literature, African-Americans have a long tradition. The first major African-American poet was Phillis Wheatley. She was a slave from Massachusetts who, in 1773, became the first black writer to publish a book. During the 1920s, an artistic movement called the Harlem Renaissance began in New York City. It included such important African-American writers as Langston Hughes and Zora Neale Hurston.

African-American author Toni Morrison is an important American writer. For her book Jazz, *she won the Nobel Prize for literature in 1993.*

In recent times, notable black writers have included Ralph Ellison, Alice Walker, and Toni Morrison. Walker, for her novel *The Color Purple,* was the first African-American to win the Pulitzer Prize in fiction. The best-known black playwright may be August Wilson, who has won many awards for his works.

Blacks have often faced prejudice in the business world. Still, many have managed to achieve great success. One of the first was Sarah Breedlove, also known as Madame C. J. Walker. In the early 1900s, her company sold hair products to African-Americans. More recently, two notable black business owners are Oprah Winfrey and Robert L. Johnson. Winfrey, the top TV talk-show host, used her popularity to build her own entertainment company, worth about $1 billion. Johnson founded Black Entertainment Television, a cable network that focuses on African-Americans. In 2000, he sold the network for about $3 billion. With his wealth, Johnson was able to buy his own professional basketball team, based in Charlotte, North Carolina. He became the first African-American to be the major owner of a professional sports team.

Jackie Robinson's strength of character and great athletic ability helped him to become the first African-American player in Major League Baseball.

For decades, though, blacks have played major roles on the nation's sports fields—once they overcame discrimination. In 1947, Jackie Robinson made history as the first black to play in baseball's major leagues. Other sports integrated in the following years. Since then, some of America's best athletes have been black. They include baseball player Willie Mays, football running back Jim Brown, and tennis star Arthur Ashe. Today, African-Americans dominate professional basketball, with Michael Jordan being perhaps the greatest player of all time. Tennis has two black stars, sisters Serena and Venus Williams. In golf, the most talented player in the world is Tiger Woods, whose racially mixed background includes African-American.

Although the arts and entertainment bring people pleasure, they cannot change a society the way politics can. During recent years, African-Americans have played a larger role in U.S. politics. Some have risen to the highest levels of the government. In 1967, civil rights lawyer Thurgood Marshall was named the first black justice on the U.S. Supreme Court. Today, Clarence Thomas sits on that court. The first African-American to serve as the head of a major government agency was Robert Weaver. He served under President Lyndon Johnson. In 2001, George W. Bush made history when he made

Sisters Venus and Serena Williams often find themselves competing against each other to determine the best player in women's tennis.

Colin Powell the country's first African-American secretary of state. In that position, Powell advises the president on foreign relations. Bush also chose an African-American woman, Condoleezza Rice, to advise him on national security. She is one of the most powerful women in the United States. The success of African-Americans such as Powell and Rice inspires Americans of all ethnic and racial backgrounds. They prove that anyone can overcome prejudice and achieve great things.

U.S. Secretary of State Colin Powell and U.S. National Security Advisor Condoleeza Rice, two powerful voices in the administration of President George W. Bush

Mid-1400s The Portuguese and Spanish begin to trade with African empires for slaves.

1539 The slave Estevanico leads Spanish explorers into what is now the southwest United States.

1619 The first Africans arrive in Virginia.

1739 A slave revolt in South Carolina kills around 60 people.

1773 Phillis Wheatley is the first African-American to publish a book.

1775–1783 Some African-American slaves win their freedom fighting in the American Revolution.

1793 The invention of the cotton gin leads to a rise in slavery in the South.

1857 In the Dred Scott case, the U.S. Supreme Court rules that African-Americans, whether free or slaves, are not U.S. citizens.

1861–1865 The Civil War divides the country, with slavery as the main issue.

1865–1877 This is the Reconstruction Era, during which slavery is abolished and African-Americans become U.S. citizens. Southern states, however, try to deny them their legal rights.

1909 W. E. B. DuBois helps found the National Association for the Advancement of Colored People (NAACP).

1914–1945 The Great Migration period, during which many blacks move from rural areas in the South to northern cities.

1920s African-American writers and artists form a movement known as the Harlem Renaissance.

1947 Jackie Robinson becomes the first African-American player in Major League Baseball.

1955 Rosa Parks refuses to give up her seat on a Montgomery, Alabama, bus, sparking the start of the civil rights movement.

1960s New laws guarantee civil rights for African Americans.

1967 Thurgood Marshall becomes the first African-American to serve on the U.S. Supreme Court.

2001 Colin Powell becomes the first African-American to serve as U.S. secretary of state; Condoleezza Rice becomes the first African-American woman to serve as U.S. national security adviser.

abolition (ab-uh-LISH-uhn)
Abolition is the immediate ending of something, such as slavery. Americans who strongly opposed slavery were known as abolitionists.

boycott (BOY-kot)
A boycott is a refusal by a large number of people to do something, such as buy a product or use a service. To fight for equal treatment, African-Americans have sometimes boycotted white businesses.

civil rights (SIV-il RITES)
The right to vote and to receive equal treatment on a job are among the civil rights that all citizens are entitled to. Since the 1940s, African-Americans have fought to guarantee their civil rights.

discrimination (diss-krim-ih-NAY-shuhn)
Discrimination is unjust behavior toward others based on such differences as race, age, nationality, or sex. African-Americans have faced discrimination ever since they first came to North America.

ethnic groups (ETH-nik GROOPS)
Ethnic groups are people from similar cultural backgrounds. These groups are usually part of a minority in the population.

indentured servants (in-DEN-shurd SUR-vuhnts)
Indentured servants were people who agreed to work for another person for a number of years. After that time was up, they were free to work and live on their own. In the 1600s, some Africans came to North America as indentured servants.

inferior (in-FEER-ee-ur)
Inferior means not as good as someone or something else. Many white Americans believed African-Americans were inferior.

inoculation (in-ok-yuh-LAY-shun)
With an inoculation, a doctor takes a small amount of bodily fluid from a sick person and gives it to healthy people. The inoculation prevents the healthy people from catching a deadly form of some diseases. African slaves showed Americans how to use inoculations to prevent the spread of smallpox.

integrate (IN-teh-grayt)
To integrate is to mix people from different backgrounds in the same building or community. The civil rights movement forced southern states to integrate, which allowed African-Americans to use the same services as whites.

minorities (muh-NOR-ih-tees)
Minorities are groups of people who make up less than half of a population. African-Americans are one of several minority groups in the United States, along with Hispanics, Asians, and Native Americans.

plantation (plan-TAY-shuhn)
A plantation was a large farm where usually one major crop, such as cotton, was raised. Most plantations were in the South, and African-American slaves did most of the work on them.

prejudice (PREJ-uh-diss)
Prejudice is the hatred or unfair treatment of others based on such differences as nationality or race. Even after slavery ended, many African-Americans faced prejudice in their daily lives.

rituals (RICH-oo-uhls)
Acts that are repeated as part of celebrations or religious services are called rituals. Some African rituals survived in the new African-American culture created by slaves.

segregated (SEG-ruh-gayt-ed)
People separated into different groups because of such differences as race or religion are said to be segregated. After the Civil War, southern states segregated blacks and whites in public buildings.

Web Sites

Visit our homepage for lots of links about African Americans:
http://www.childsworld.com/links.html

Note to Parents, Teachers, and Librarians:
We routinely verify our Web links to make sure they're safe,
active sites—so encourage your readers to check them out!

Books

Bel Monte, Kathryn. *African-American Heroes & Heroines.* Hollywood, Fla.: Lifetime Books, 1998.

Meadows, James. *Slavery: The Struggle for Freedom.* Chanhassen, Minn.: Child's World, 2002.

Tate, Eleanora E. *African American Musicians.* New York: Wiley, 2000.

Venable, Rose. *The Civil Rights Movement.* Chanhassen, Minn.: Child's World, 2001.

Welch, Catherine A. *Children of the Civil Rights Movement.* Minneapolis: Carolrhoda Books, 2001.

Places to Visit or Contact

National Civil Rights Museum
450 Mulberry Street
Memphis, TN 38103
901/521-9699

Charles H. Wright Museum of African-American History
315 E. Warren Avenue
Detroit, MI 48201-1443
313/494-5800

National Museum of African Art
950 Independence Avenue, S.W.
Washington, D.C. 20560-0708
202/357-4600

Index

Armstrong, Louis, 23
Ashe, Arthur, 26

Berry, Chuck, 23
Berry, Halle, 23, 24
boycotts, 21
Brown, Jim, 26
Buffalo Soldiers, 18

civil rights movement, 18,
    19–20, 21
Civil War, 11, 7, 16–17
Coltrane, John, 23
Constitution, 7, 17–18
Cosby, Bill, 24
cotton, 8, 12–13

Davis, Miles, 23
Davis, Ossie, 24
discrimination, 7, 20, 26
Douglass, Frederick, 13
DuBois, W. E. B., 19

Ellington, Duke, 23
Ellison, Ralph, 25
Emancipation Proclamation, 17
escaped slaves, 12, 13–14, 17

farming, 8, 10, 19
foods, 11

Gates, Henry Louis, Jr., 25

Hughes, Langston, 24
Hurston, Zora Neale, 24

immigrants, 6–7
integration, 20, 26

Jackson, Jesse, 21
Jackson, Samuel L., 24
Jamestown, Virginia, 8
Jay-Z, 23
Jemison, Mae C., 27
"Jim Crow" laws, 18–19
Johnson, Robert, 22–23
Johnson, Robert L., 25
Jones, James Earl, 24
Jordan, Michael, 26

King, Martin Luther, Jr., 21

Lincoln, Abraham, 16, 17
literature, 24–25
Love, Nat, 18

Marsalis, Wynton, 23
Marshall, Thurgood, 27
Mays, Willie, 26
Mitchell, Brian Stokes, 24
Morrison, Toni, 24, 25
music, 10, 22–23

NAACP, 19, 20

Parker, Charlie, 22, 23
Parks, Rosa, 21
politics, 18, 27–28
Powell, Colin, 28
prejudice, 7, 15, 19

Redman, Joshua, 23
religion, 11
Rice, Condoleezza, 28
Ringgold, Faith, 20
Robinson, Jackie, 26

Scott, Dred, 14
segregation, 18, 20
Shakur, Tupac, 23
slavery, 7–9, 10,
    11, 12–13, 14, 16
Smith, Bessie, 22
sports, 25–26
Supreme Court, 14, 18, 20, 27

Thomas, Clarence, 27
tobacco, 8, 10
Truth, Sojourner, 17
Tubman, Harriet, 14
Tuskegee Airmen, 19

Vereen, Ben, 24

Walker, Alice, 25
Walker, Madame C. J., 25
Washington, Denzel, 23, 24
Weaver, Robert, 27
Wheatley, Phillis, 24
Williams, Serena and Venus, 26, 27
Wilson, August, 25
Winfrey, Oprah, 25
Woods, Tiger, 26

About the Author

MICHAEL BURGAN IS A FREELANCE WRITER OF BOOKS FOR CHILDREN and adults. A history graduate of the University of Connecticut, he has written more than 60 fiction and nonfiction children's books for various publishers. For adult audiences, he has written news articles, essays, and plays. Michael Burgan is a recipient of an Edpress Award and belongs to the Society of Children's Book Writers and Illustrators.